will the wolf

Will sits and watches the world go by, feeling all alone. Will he be alone forever?

This picture book targets the /w/ sound and is part of *Speech Bubbles 2*, a series of picture books that target specific speech sounds within the story.

The series can be used for children receiving speech therapy, for children who have a speech sound delay/disorder, or simply as an activity for children's speech sound development and/or phonological awareness. They are ideal for use by parents, teachers or caregivers.

Bright pictures and a fun story create an engaging activity perfect for sound awareness.

Picture books are sold individually, or in a pack. There are currently two packs available – *Speech Bubbles 1* and *Speech Bubbles 2.* Please see further titles in the series for stories targeting other speech sounds.

Melissa Palmer is a Speech Language Therapist. She worked for the Ministry of Education, Special Education in New Zealand from 2008 to 2013, with children aged primarily between 2 and 8 years of age. She also completed a diploma in children's writing in 2009, studying under author Janice Marriott, through the New Zealand Business Institute. Melissa has a passion for articulation and phonology, as well as writing and art, and has combined these two loves to create *Speech Bubbles*.

T0276913

What's in the pack?

User Guide

Vinnie the Dove

Rick's Carrot

Harry the Hopper

Have You Ever Met a Yeti?

Zack the Buzzy Bee

Asher the Thresher Shark

Catch That Chicken!

Will the Wolf

Magic Licking Lollipops

Jasper the Badger

Platypus and Fly

The Dragon Drawing War

Will the Wolf

Targeting the /w/ Sound

Melissa Palmer

Routledge
Taylor & Francis Group

LONDON AND NEW YORK

First published 2021
by Routledge
2 Park Square, Milton Park, Abingdon, Oxon OX14 4RN

and by Routledge
52 Vanderbilt Avenue, New York, NY 10017

Routledge is an imprint of the Taylor & Francis Group, an informa business

British Library Cataloguing-in-Publication Data
A catalogue record for this book is available from the British Library

Library of Congress Cataloging-in-Publication Data
A catalog record has been requested for this book

ISBN: 978-1-138-59784-6 (set)
ISBN: 978-0-367-64878-7 (pbk)
ISBN: 978-1-003-12672-0 (ebk)

Typeset in Calibri
by Newgen Publishing UK

will the wolf

Will the **w**olf loved to **w**atch all the **w**orld g**oi**ng on around him.

When it rained, making his fur all **w**et – he **w**atched.

When it **w**as **w**indy, he **w**ent behind a **w**ood pile – and he **w**atched.

When it **w**as sunny and hot, he lapped some **w**ater – and still he **w**atched.

He **w**atched a man **w**heel a**w**ay a **w**agon full of **w**eeds.

He **w**atched a **w**orm **w**iggle out of a puddle of **w**ater.

Will **w**atched **w**et clothes blo**w**ing in the **w**ind on a **w**ashing line.

He **w**atched **w**hales playing in the **w**aves of the sea.

And **w**hile he **w**atched, **W**ill was filled **w**ith **w**onder at **w**hat a magical **w**orld he lived in. There **w**as only **o**ne problem **w**ith his **w**onderful life – he **w**as very lonely. He didn't have any other **w**olves in his family. He **w**as all alone.

One day, **w**hile **W**ill the **w**olf **w**atched, he saw another **w**olf sneaking a**w**ay into the night. Still a**w**ake, he decided to follow the **w**olf to see **w**hat it **w**as up to.

The **w**olf had beautiful **w**hite fur and po**w**erful eyes, as she sat on the hill, looking up at the bright moon.

"Who are you, and **w**hat are you doing?" **W**ill asked the **w**olf.

"My name is **W**illa," the **w**olf said. "I just love **w**atching the moon." And then she howled.

O-w-w-w-w-w-w-w-w-w-w-w-w-w-w-w-w-

It **w**as a magical sound, and **W**ill couldn't resist – he had to join in.

O-w-w-w-w-w-w-w-w-w-w-w-w-w-w-w-w-w-

Together, **W**ill and **W**illa **w**atched the moon, and became friends.

Will was no longer lonely – he had his very own friend to **w**atch the **w**orld **w**ith – and howl **w**ith too!